Living GOD's *Grace*

The Journey Continues

Deborah Harris Christopher

Living God's Grace

Copyright © 2020 by Deborah Harris Christopher

ISBN:9798676635336 (Paperback)

Printed in the United States of America

"Living God's Grace" is dedicated to my husband
Ralph B. Christopher, Jr. and my son Ethan
Garrett Christopher. Thanking God for
their endless love and support.

Contents

# Contents

Trust in the Lord with all
thine heart; and lean not
unto thine own understanding.
In all thy ways acknowledge him,
And he shall direct thy paths.
Proverbs 3:5,6, KJV

Epigraph

**God continues to use me as a vessel
to convey His messages.**

Acknowledgement

Glory to God who is the head of my life, who continues to use me. As many of you may already know, "Living God's Grace" is my second book of poetry. Both books contain life messages that are conveyed through poetry.

I would like to thank all who purchased my first book, "Daily Living through God's Grace". Your patronage to me means more to me than I could ever express to you. I feel especially honored that many of you let me know that you really did enjoy the book.

I was given many opportunities to re-write "Daily Living through God's Grace", but declined. The reasoning was to create a book that was more cost efficient. My final decision was to write another book of poetry containing new poems and a few of the more popular poems from the first book.

Again, thanks to all who purchased my first book. May God continue to richly bless each of you.

Introduction

My journey began more than twenty-five years ago when I was in a very dark place. I was in need of a physical and spiritual healing. Deep in Depression, along with other health issues, there was a need for a spiritual cleansing that only God could provide. That relationship with God, kept me during the dark days and has transformed me into the woman of God that I am today.

My first book "Daily Living through God's Grace", was written during my dark times when the Lord would speak to me through poems and writings. This began over a sixteen-year period. I would just write, and during that sixteen-year period, many of the poems changed, and so did I. It was then that I was instructed by God to write "Daily Living through God's Grace". There were poems that lifted me up out of my Depression, and my transformation began.

"Living God's Grace" is a continuation of my journey with God. This book does contain some of my most popular poems that were used in the first book. These poems highly emphasize the two main subjects of great importance. Those subjects are struggles and guidance, because God emphasizes with great concern the struggles that Christians face and the guidance needed to face those struggles. Daily struggles are things that all Christians must learn to master. Mastering those pains only comes from much needed guidance in order to successfully navigate us through this sin filled world.

Chapter 1

Life's Struggles

A wrathful man stirreth
up strife: but he that is slow
to anger appeaseth strife.
Proverbs 15:18, KJV

When I'm not Happy

When I'm not happy it is easy to see,
the hurt and pain of the inner me.
I know that I should look for
the best, and not the worst,
but at times, life is full of hurt.
How can you be happy, when I'm not?
It seems that hurt and pain is all I've got.
When I'm not happy, there is no illusion,
my pain brings about much
turmoil and confusion.
Life is not perfect, something
we all must face.

We must always remember that no
matter how bad things are going,
there is nothing that is too hard for God.
Because He has all power in His hands,
you just need to give your hurt to Him.
God will change your frown,
by turning things around.
Live life to the fullest and do
not let your life go to waste.

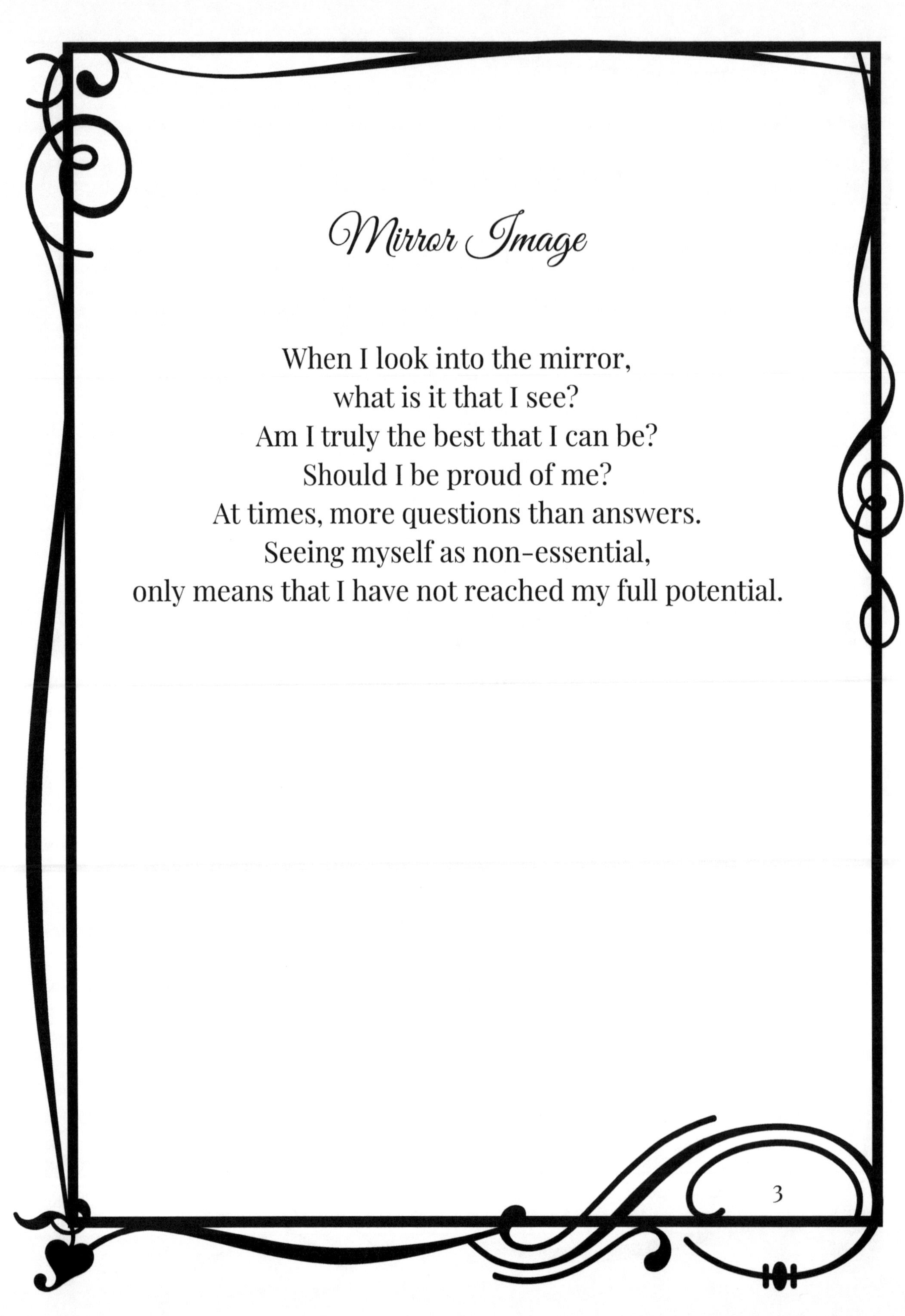

Mirror Image

When I look into the mirror,
what is it that I see?
Am I truly the best that I can be?
Should I be proud of me?
At times, more questions than answers.
Seeing myself as non-essential,
only means that I have not reached my full potential.

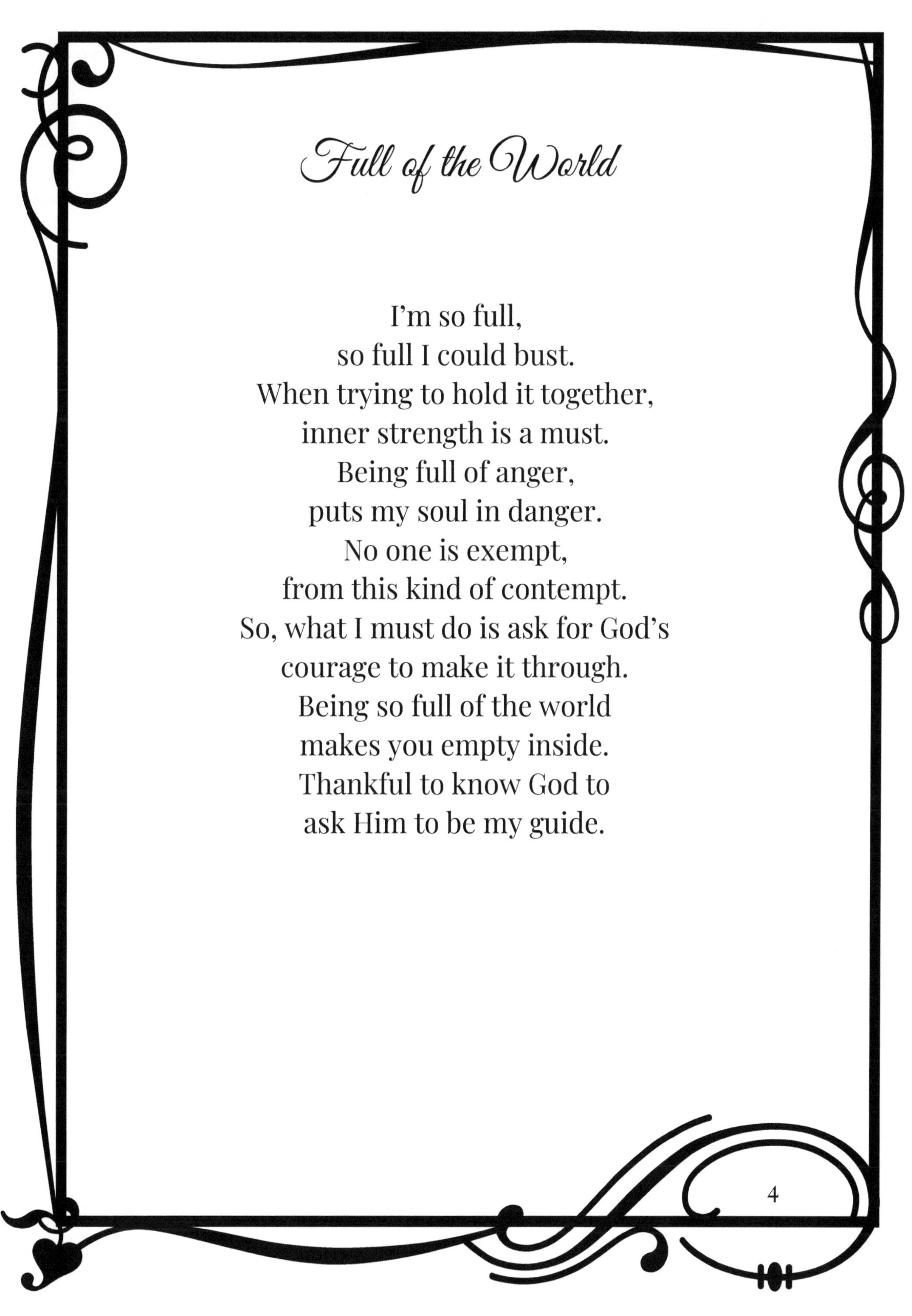

Full of the World

I'm so full,
so full I could bust.
When trying to hold it together,
inner strength is a must.
Being full of anger,
puts my soul in danger.
No one is exempt,
from this kind of contempt.
So, what I must do is ask for God's
courage to make it through.
Being so full of the world
makes you empty inside.
Thankful to know God to
ask Him to be my guide.

The Fist

The fist balled tight,
careful to not let anything out.
Busy to not let go of anything,
but also blocking a way to get something.
The fist all nice and tight,
determined to not do what's right.

God commands us to love thy neighbor as thyself.

The Lost Generation

I grieve for what they will never achieve.
They have access to the best technology, with
opportunities we could only dream of.

Who are they?
They are our children.
The lost generation.

Lost because we were too blind to see.
With the highly skilled knowledge of
modern technology, they are still lacking.
Our children lack basic communication skills.
Sure, they easily navigate phones,
emails, and social media.
However, they lack face to face
communication with other people.
A whole generation in the wilderness.
Where did we go wrong?
They are lost because we were too blind
to see what is really important in the world.

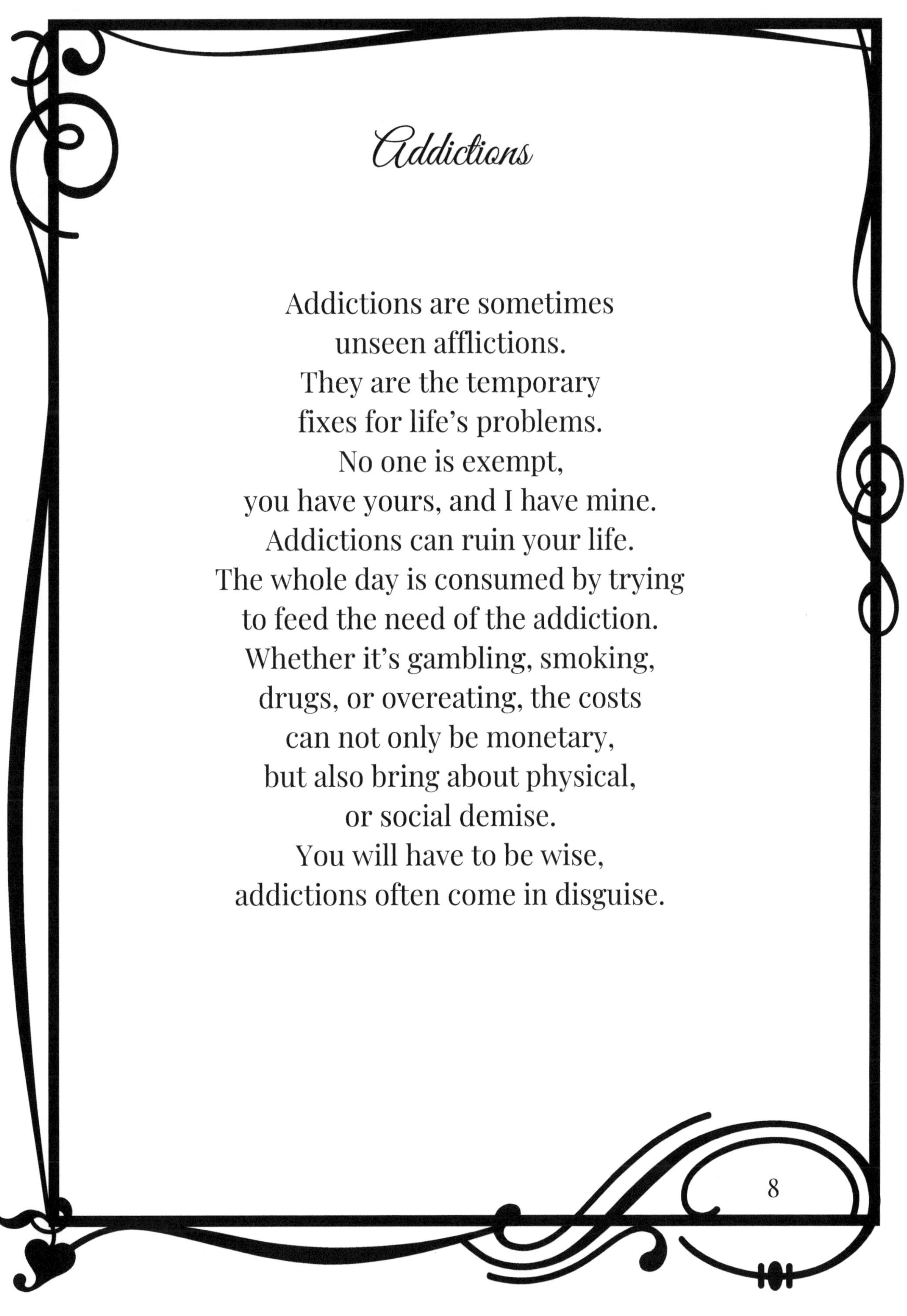

Addictions

Addictions are sometimes
unseen afflictions.
They are the temporary
fixes for life's problems.
No one is exempt,
you have yours, and I have mine.
Addictions can ruin your life.
The whole day is consumed by trying
to feed the need of the addiction.
Whether it's gambling, smoking,
drugs, or overeating, the costs
can not only be monetary,
but also bring about physical,
or social demise.
You will have to be wise,
addictions often come in disguise.

Me Mentality

The me mentality is all about me,
not helping anyone, not even family.
The word is selfish, and when you are selfish,
not much will you accomplish.

You come into this world, and leave it alone,
but in living you can't do it on your own.
Life is about give and take, and without giving,
there is not much of an impression you will make.

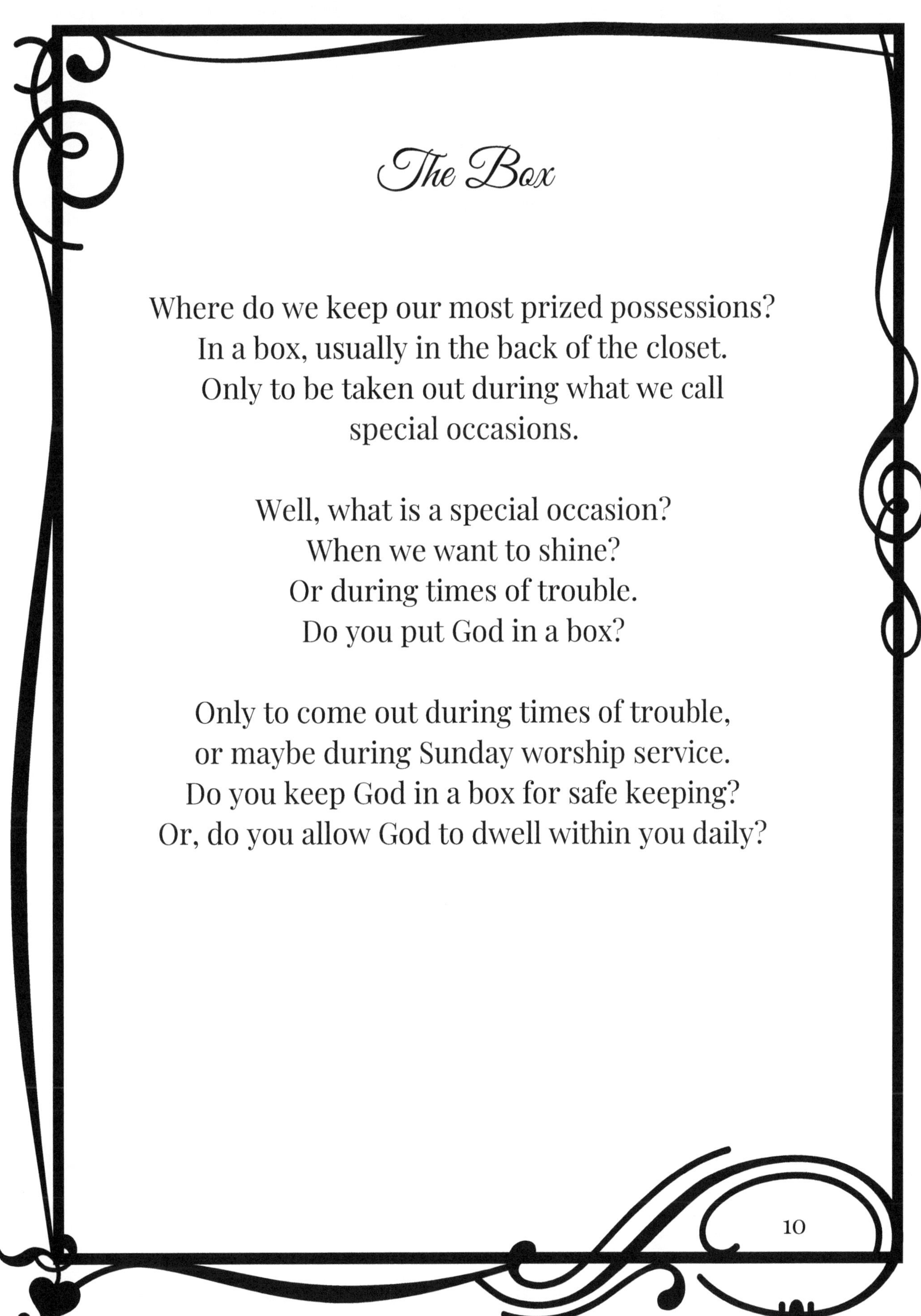

The Box

Where do we keep our most prized possessions?
In a box, usually in the back of the closet.
Only to be taken out during what we call
special occasions.

Well, what is a special occasion?
When we want to shine?
Or during times of trouble.
Do you put God in a box?

Only to come out during times of trouble,
or maybe during Sunday worship service.
Do you keep God in a box for safe keeping?
Or, do you allow God to dwell within you daily?

Be sweet, give a smile to
everyone you meet.

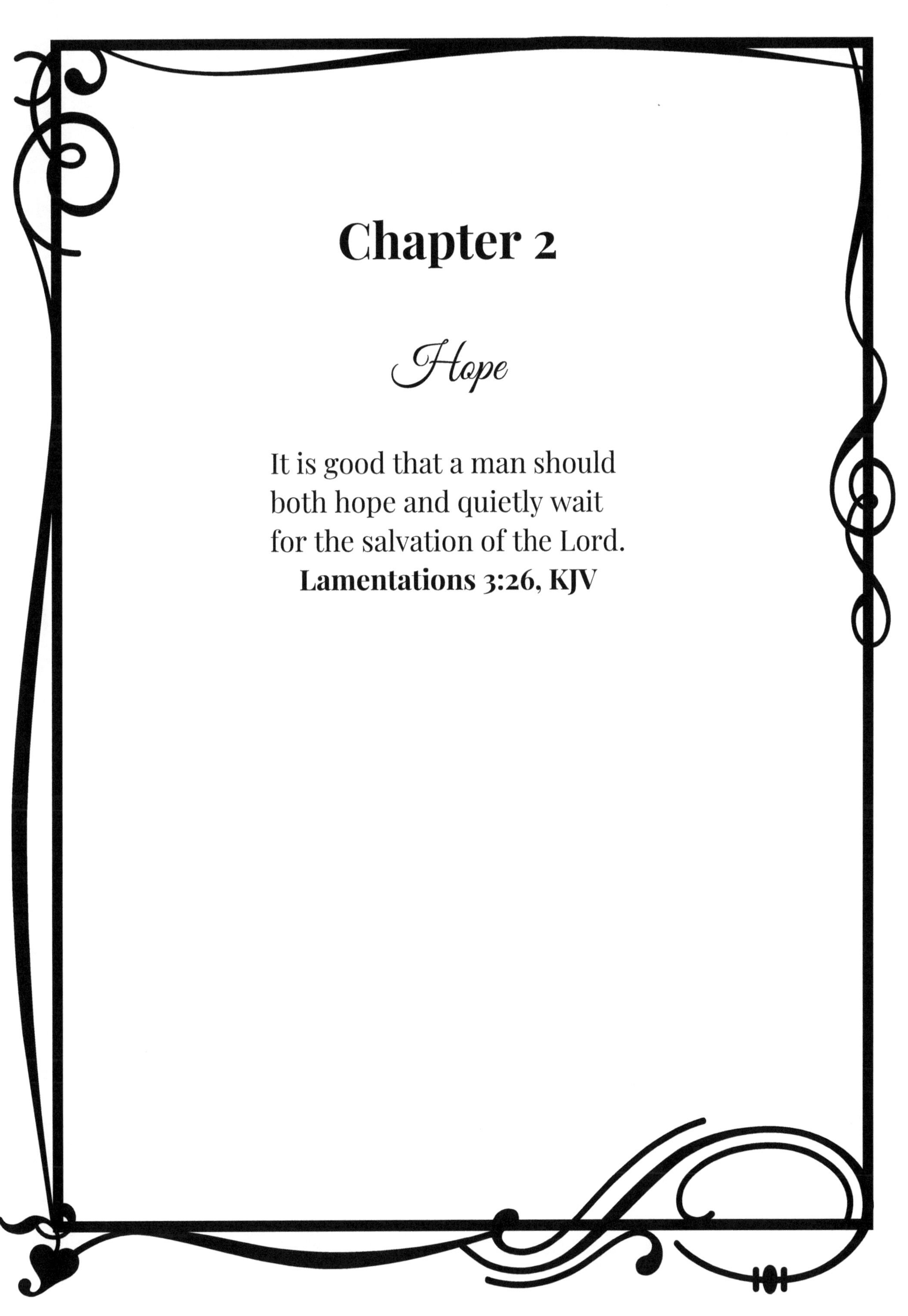

Chapter 2

Hope

It is good that a man should
both hope and quietly wait
for the salvation of the Lord.
Lamentations 3:26, KJV

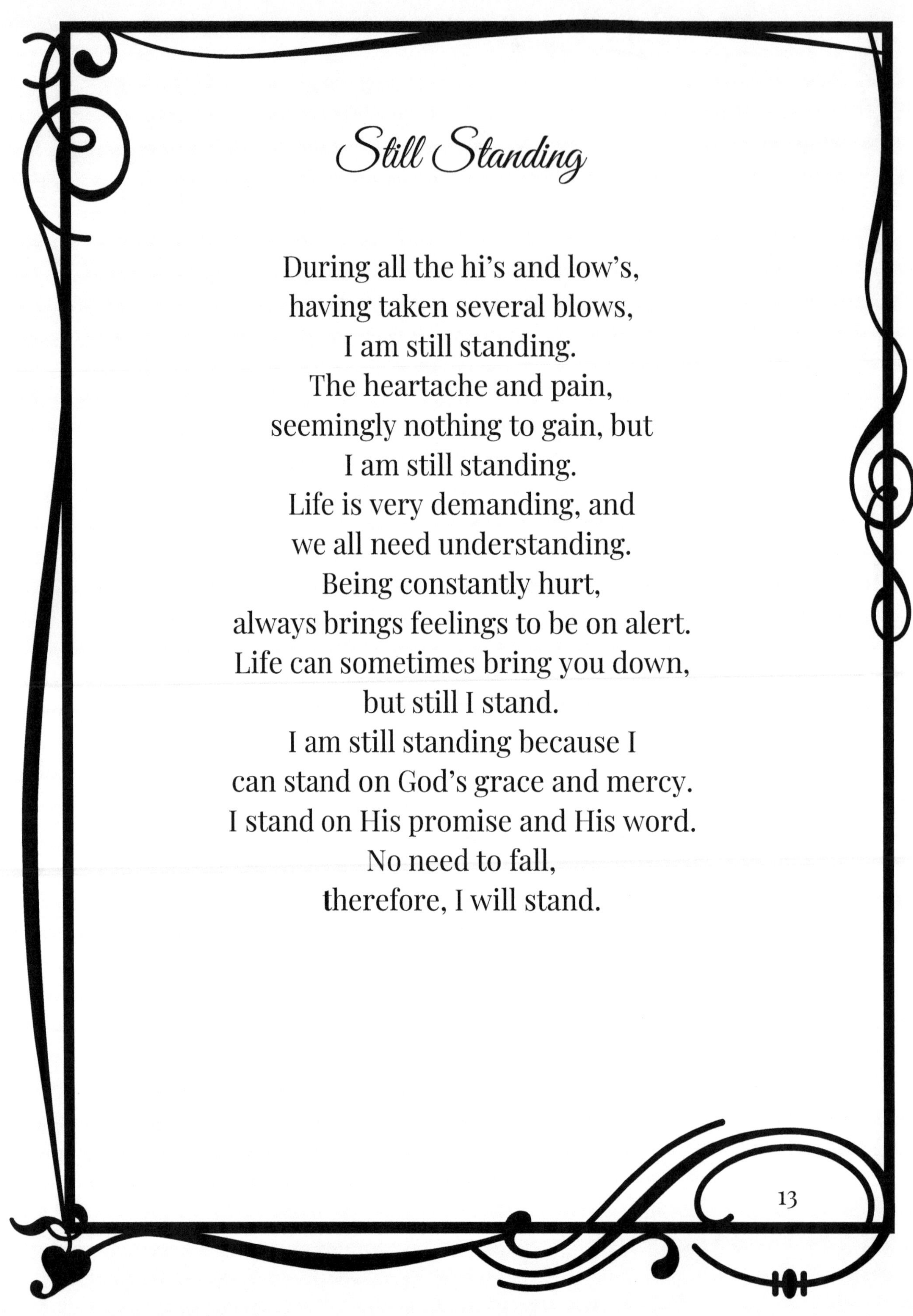

Still Standing

During all the hi's and low's,
having taken several blows,
I am still standing.
The heartache and pain,
seemingly nothing to gain, but
I am still standing.
Life is very demanding, and
we all need understanding.
Being constantly hurt,
always brings feelings to be on alert.
Life can sometimes bring you down,
but still I stand.
I am still standing because I
can stand on God's grace and mercy.
I stand on His promise and His word.
No need to fall,
therefore, I will stand.

Stay on the Path

Stay on the path another day.
Stay on the path because it
is going to be a brighter day.
Just to ruin the flow,
distractions will come and go.
We stay on the path,
to avoid God's wrath.
All people of God
let us stay on the path.
God's way is the right way,
He does ask you to
do this each and every day.

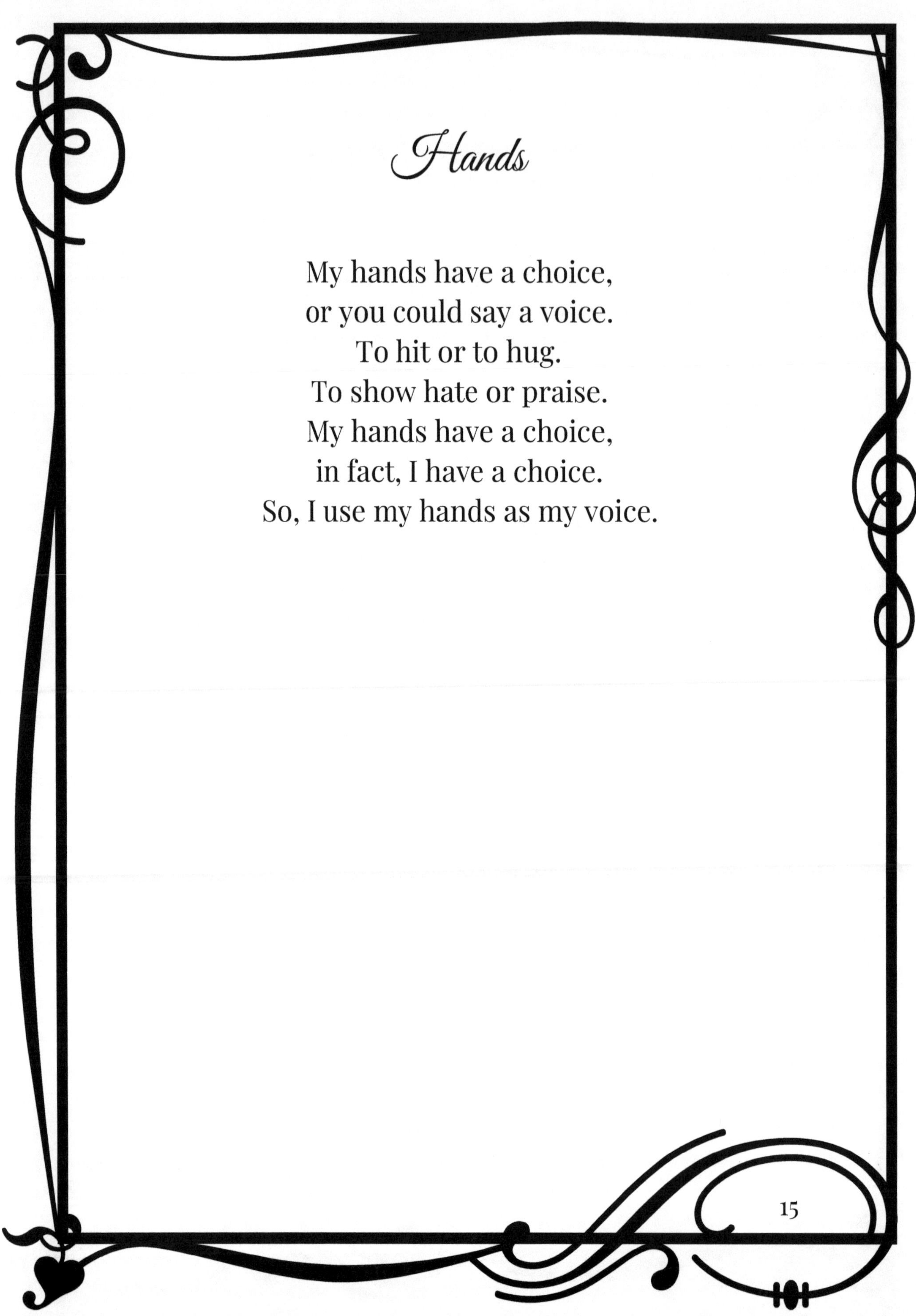

Hands

My hands have a choice,
or you could say a voice.
To hit or to hug.
To show hate or praise.
My hands have a choice,
in fact, I have a choice.
So, I use my hands as my voice.

Step by Step

Step by step,
Lord, I need your help.
Please lift me up and
surround me with your
love and understanding.
Life is hard, and I
don't know what to do.
So I look to you Lord,
please show me the way,
step by step each
and every day.

Allow your sins to drown in God's sea of forgiveness.

The Lone Christian

Sometimes I feel like a lone Christian.
Alone because there appears to
be no one else to
feel my pains of the world.
Trying to live right seems to be in vain.
Many fellow Christians seem
to follow the world.
Although I do feel alone, I
know that I'm not on my own.
God is with me, and I just have
to make His presence known.

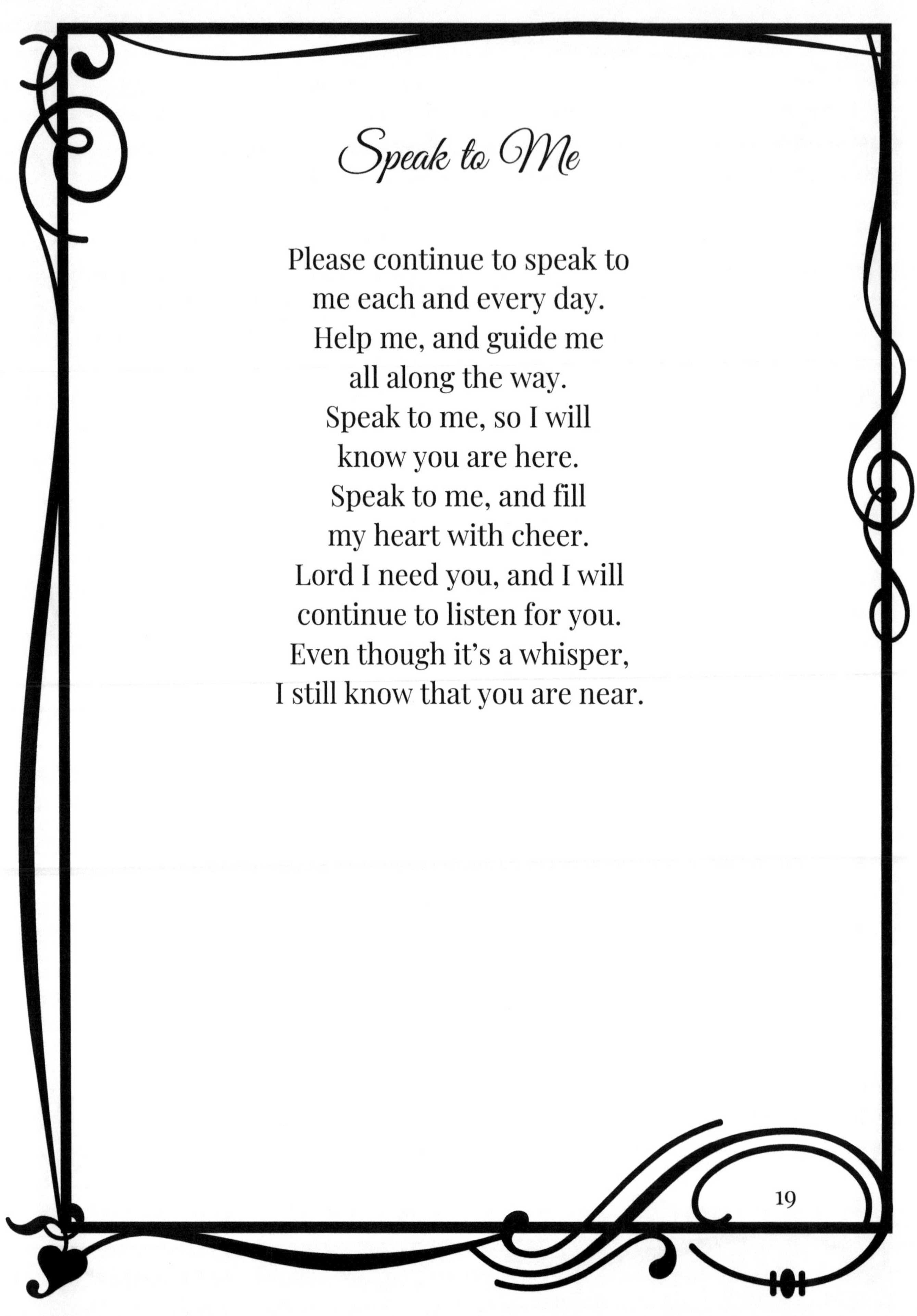

Speak to Me

Please continue to speak to
me each and every day.
Help me, and guide me
all along the way.
Speak to me, so I will
know you are here.
Speak to me, and fill
my heart with cheer.
Lord I need you, and I will
continue to listen for you.
Even though it's a whisper,
I still know that you are near.

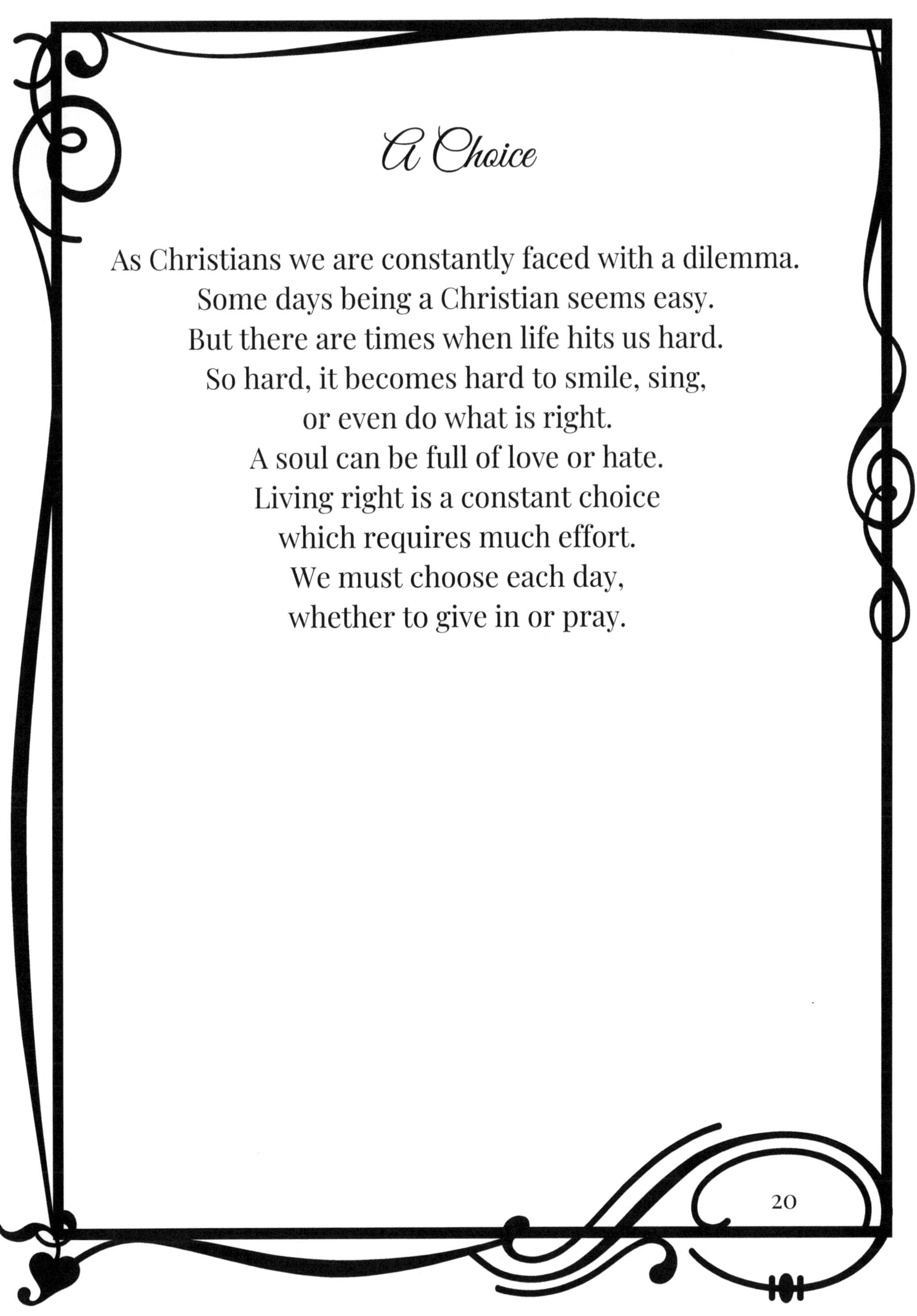

A Choice

As Christians we are constantly faced with a dilemma.
Some days being a Christian seems easy.
But there are times when life hits us hard.
So hard, it becomes hard to smile, sing,
or even do what is right.
A soul can be full of love or hate.
Living right is a constant choice
which requires much effort.
We must choose each day,
whether to give in or pray.

Build me Up

Build me up and cleanse my soul,
make my spirit pure as gold.
The world is full of sin,
and temptation will come again.
Anger, bitterness, loss, and betrayal
all takes hold of me.
Recovery is hard to perceive.
Please build me up, and cleanse my soul,
only God can recover me whole.
I've been tired, and I've been weak,
only God's love can be so sweet.

The faith of a mustard seed is all you will need to succeed.

Chapter 3

Encouragement

For his anger endureth but a moment;
in his favor is life: weeping may endure
for a night, but joy
cometh in the morning.
Psalm 30:5, KJV

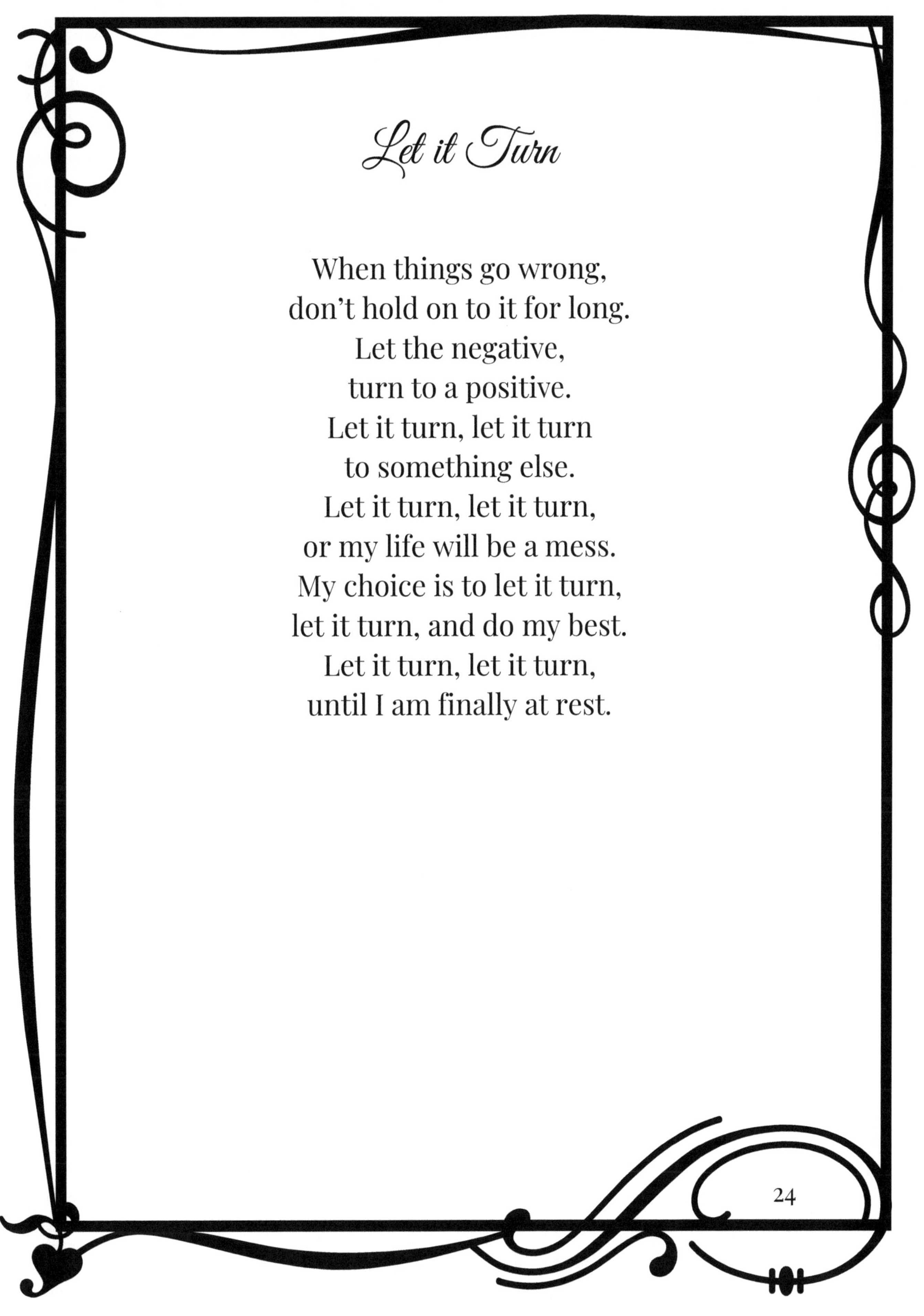

Let it Turn

When things go wrong,
don't hold on to it for long.
Let the negative,
turn to a positive.
Let it turn, let it turn
to something else.
Let it turn, let it turn,
or my life will be a mess.
My choice is to let it turn,
let it turn, and do my best.
Let it turn, let it turn,
until I am finally at rest.

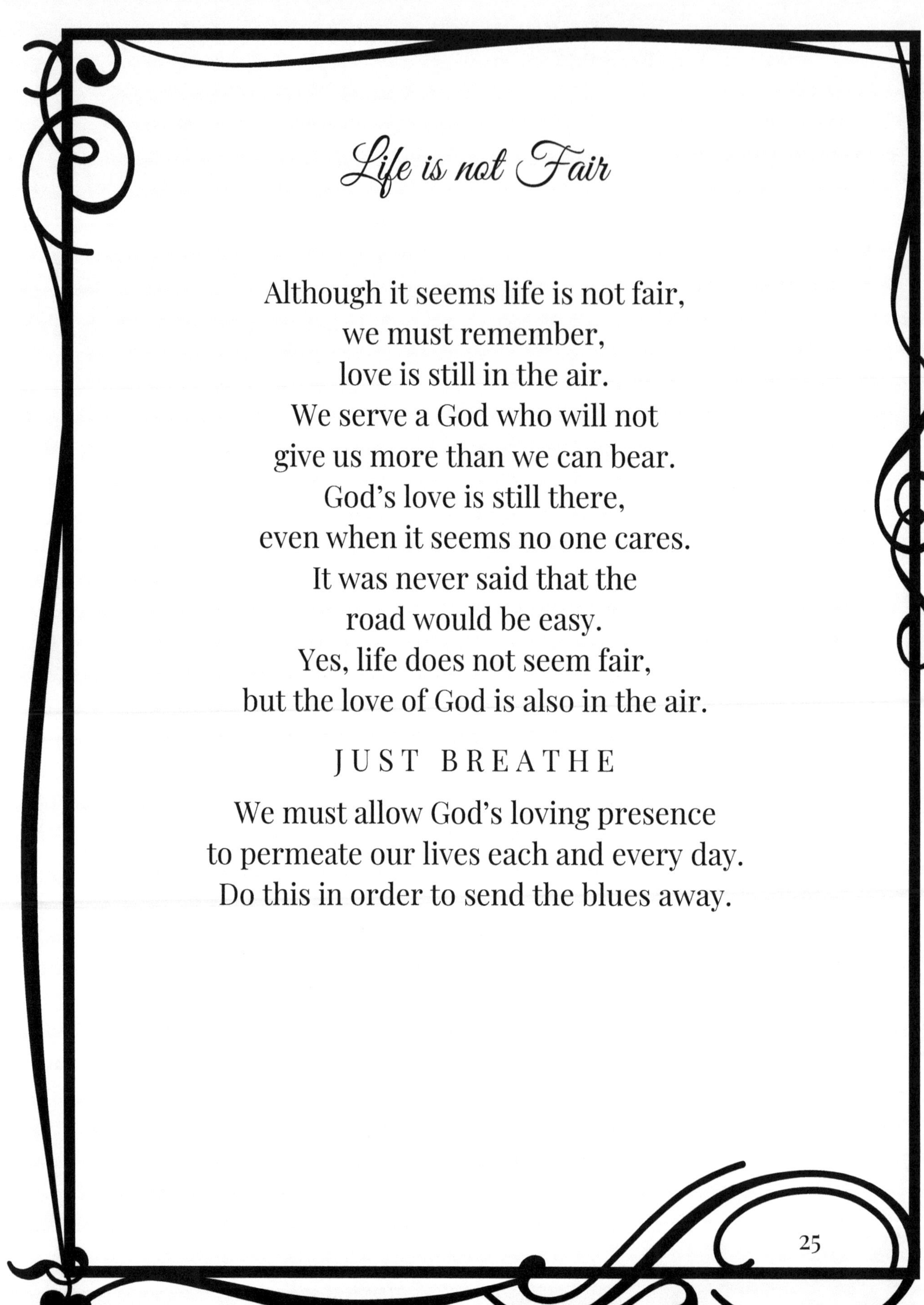

Life is not Fair

Although it seems life is not fair,
we must remember,
love is still in the air.
We serve a God who will not
give us more than we can bear.
God's love is still there,
even when it seems no one cares.
It was never said that the
road would be easy.
Yes, life does not seem fair,
but the love of God is also in the air.

JUST BREATHE

We must allow God's loving presence
to permeate our lives each and every day.
Do this in order to send the blues away.

Smile

A smile may be just the thing to make
someone's day bright.
Smiles emulate love and acceptance.
A smile has the possibility
of changing a person's mood.
Smiles are non-verbal cues that
are easily understood.

Why Me?

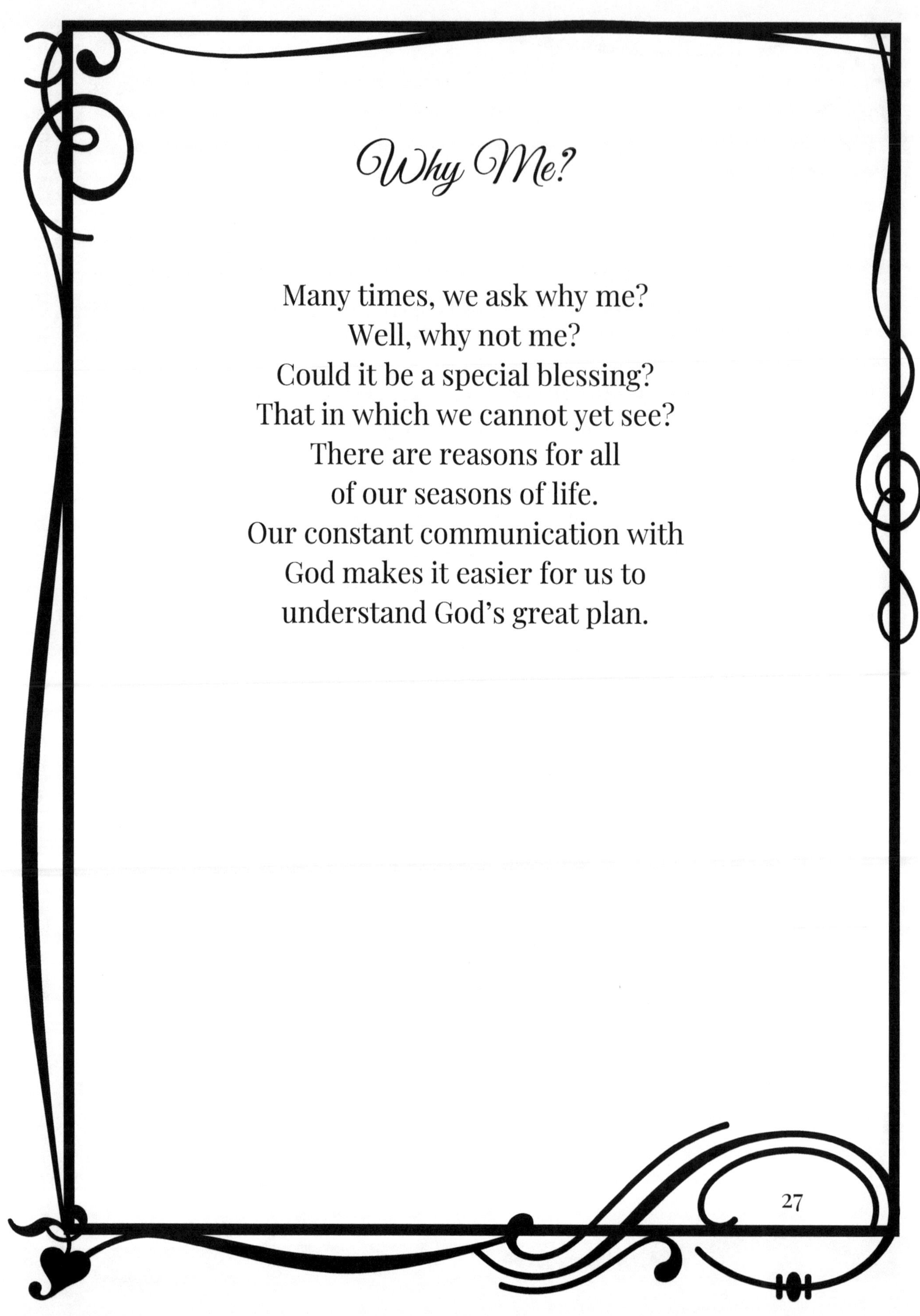

Many times, we ask why me?
Well, why not me?
Could it be a special blessing?
That in which we cannot yet see?
There are reasons for all
of our seasons of life.
Our constant communication with
God makes it easier for us to
understand God's great plan.

God not only loves us constantly, but unconditionally.

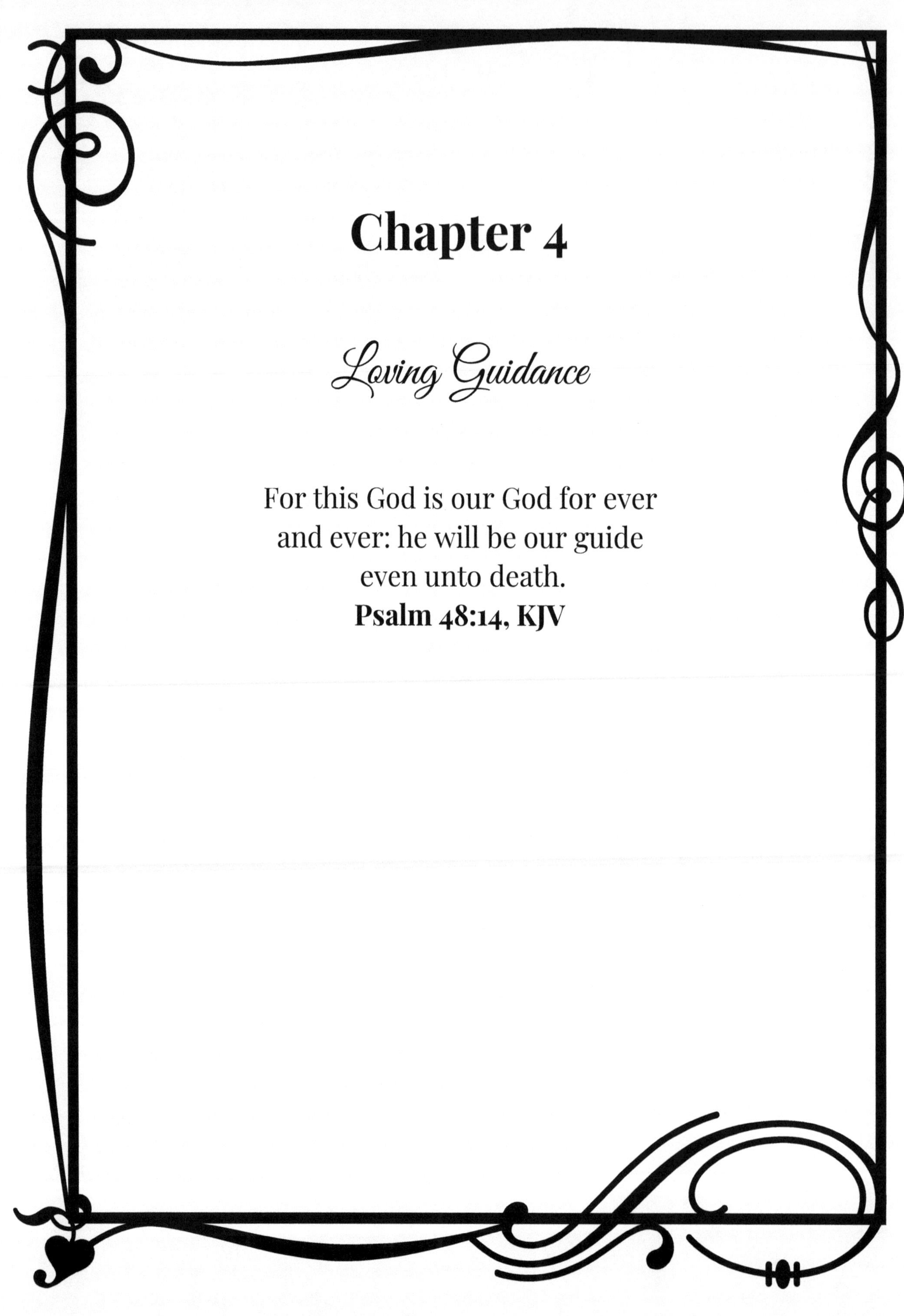

Chapter 4

Loving Guidance

For this God is our God for ever
and ever: he will be our guide
even unto death.
Psalm 48:14, KJV

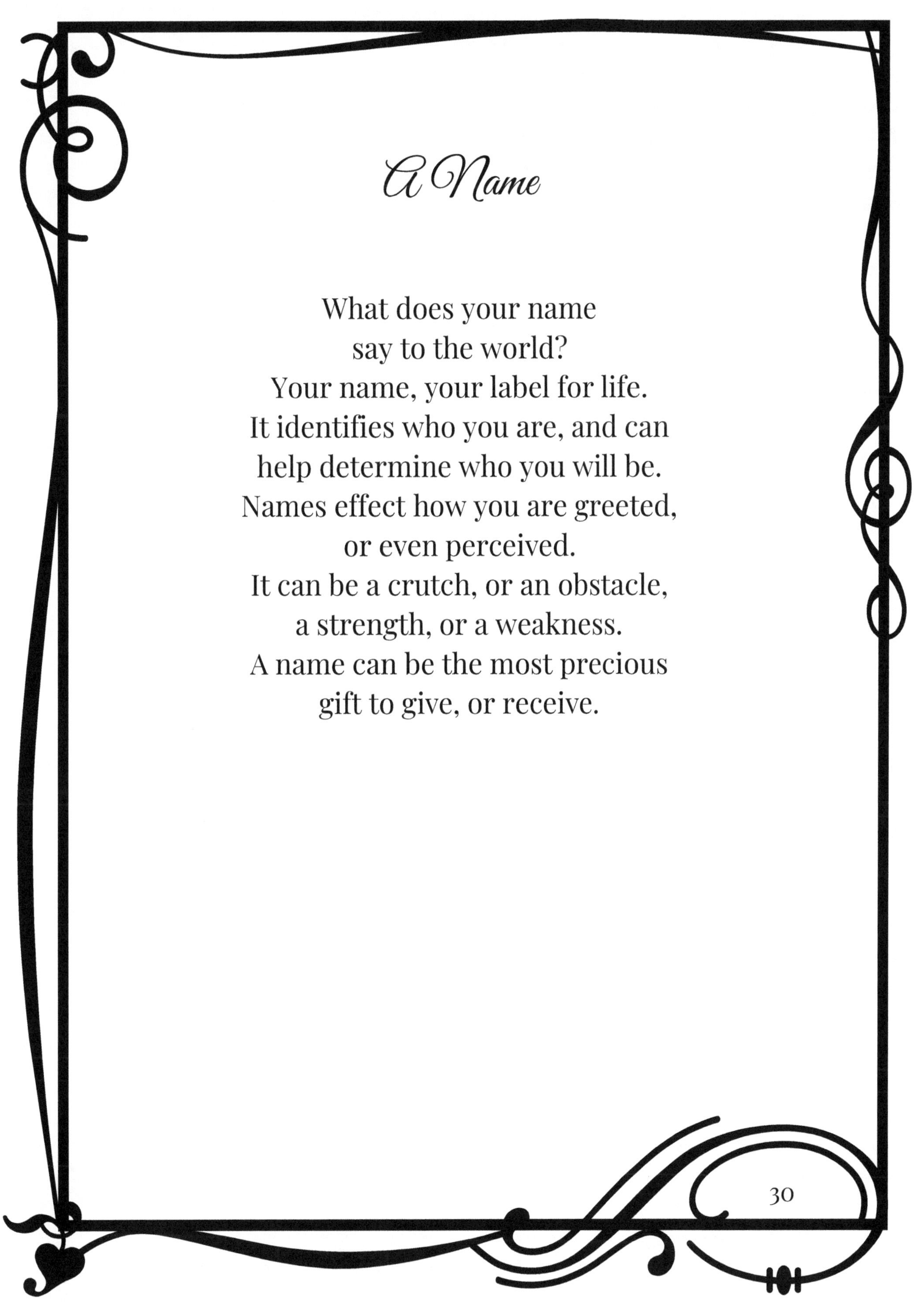

A Name

What does your name
say to the world?
Your name, your label for life.
It identifies who you are, and can
help determine who you will be.
Names effect how you are greeted,
or even perceived.
It can be a crutch, or an obstacle,
a strength, or a weakness.
A name can be the most precious
gift to give, or receive.

Be a Man

Be a man like only you can.
No one looks at a baby boy, and says he is going to grow
up to be a drug dealer, child molester,
rapist, or gigolo.
The expectations are high, and should remain high.
High expectations do require a lot of work.
Growing up without the proper father figure can make a
boy a man or a fool.
Young men you must break the cycle.
There is no excuse to spiral down society as the image of a
respectable man becomes a myth.
To be a man, one must first love God, and himself.
If you can achieve these two things, then the task is easy.
Life situations can make this task easier for some than
others, but nonetheless, can still be achieved.

This is a challenge to all young men and boys, to love God
and himself.

The Pain of a Gain

Before you succeed or make progress,
Satan is always there with his mess.
He keeps you bound,
and tries to turn you around.
It never fails, before there is success,
you will experience some pain.
The more it hurts,
the higher the worth.
Life is hard, and nothing comes easy.
Just remember before your gain,
you will feel some pain.

Grief

In life, I have had enough sorrow,
to let others borrow.
The death of a close loved
one changes you.
You look at life differently.
Things that did not matter much,
may now not matter at all.
Perspectives change,
you change.
Grief allows us to look at life
through a different lens.

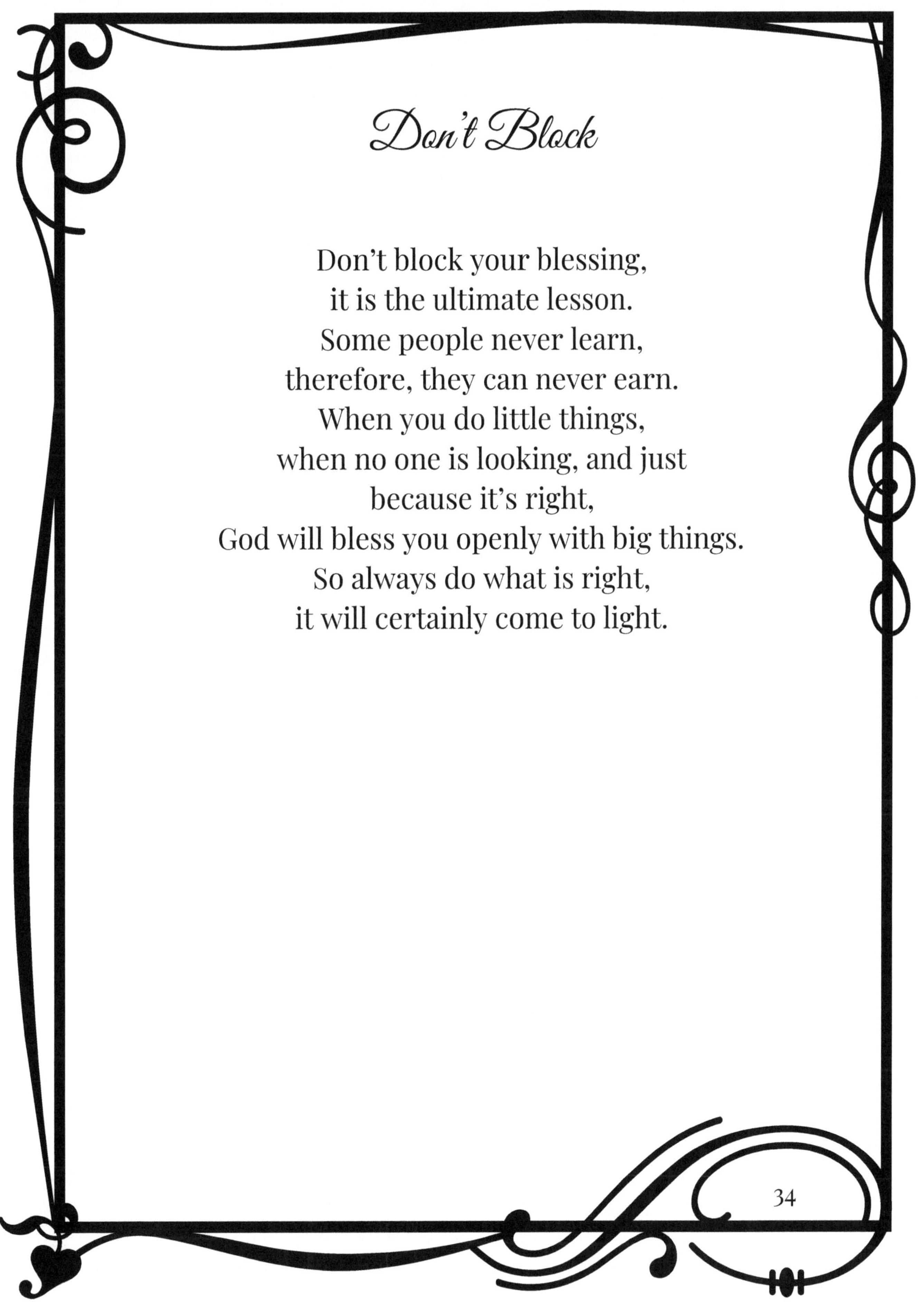

Don't Block

Don't block your blessing,
it is the ultimate lesson.
Some people never learn,
therefore, they can never earn.
When you do little things,
when no one is looking, and just
because it's right,
God will bless you openly with big things.
So always do what is right,
it will certainly come to light.

That which God binds together, He will never sever.

What makes me a Woman?

What makes me a woman?
What makes me a woman is the inner me,
that which you cannot see.
It certainly is not the amount of
physical love I share,
or the fruit I bear.

I am full of love, dignity, and grace,
which starts from within
my own inner space.

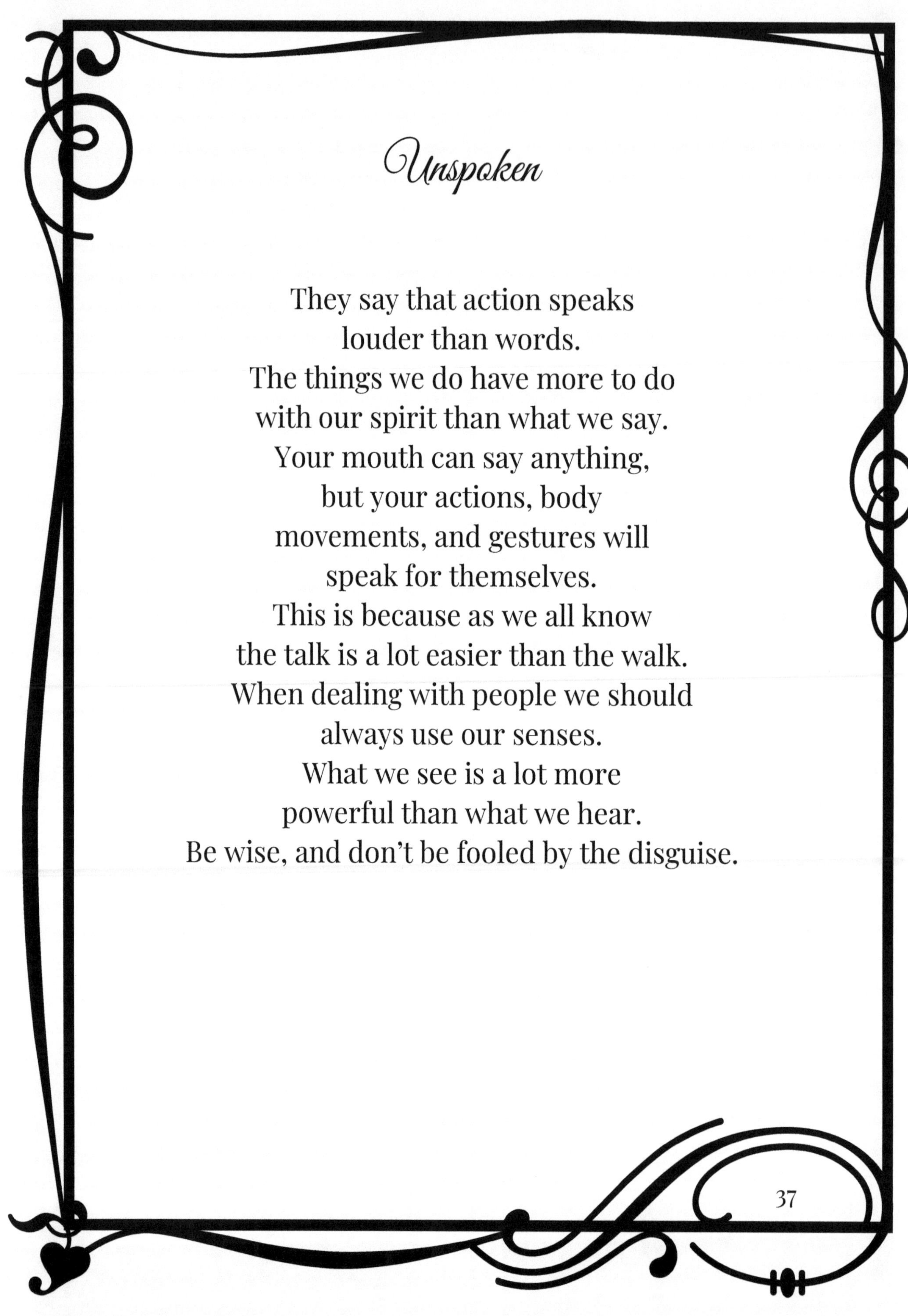

Unspoken

They say that action speaks
louder than words.
The things we do have more to do
with our spirit than what we say.
Your mouth can say anything,
but your actions, body
movements, and gestures will
speak for themselves.
This is because as we all know
the talk is a lot easier than the walk.
When dealing with people we should
always use our senses.
What we see is a lot more
powerful than what we hear.
Be wise, and don't be fooled by the disguise.

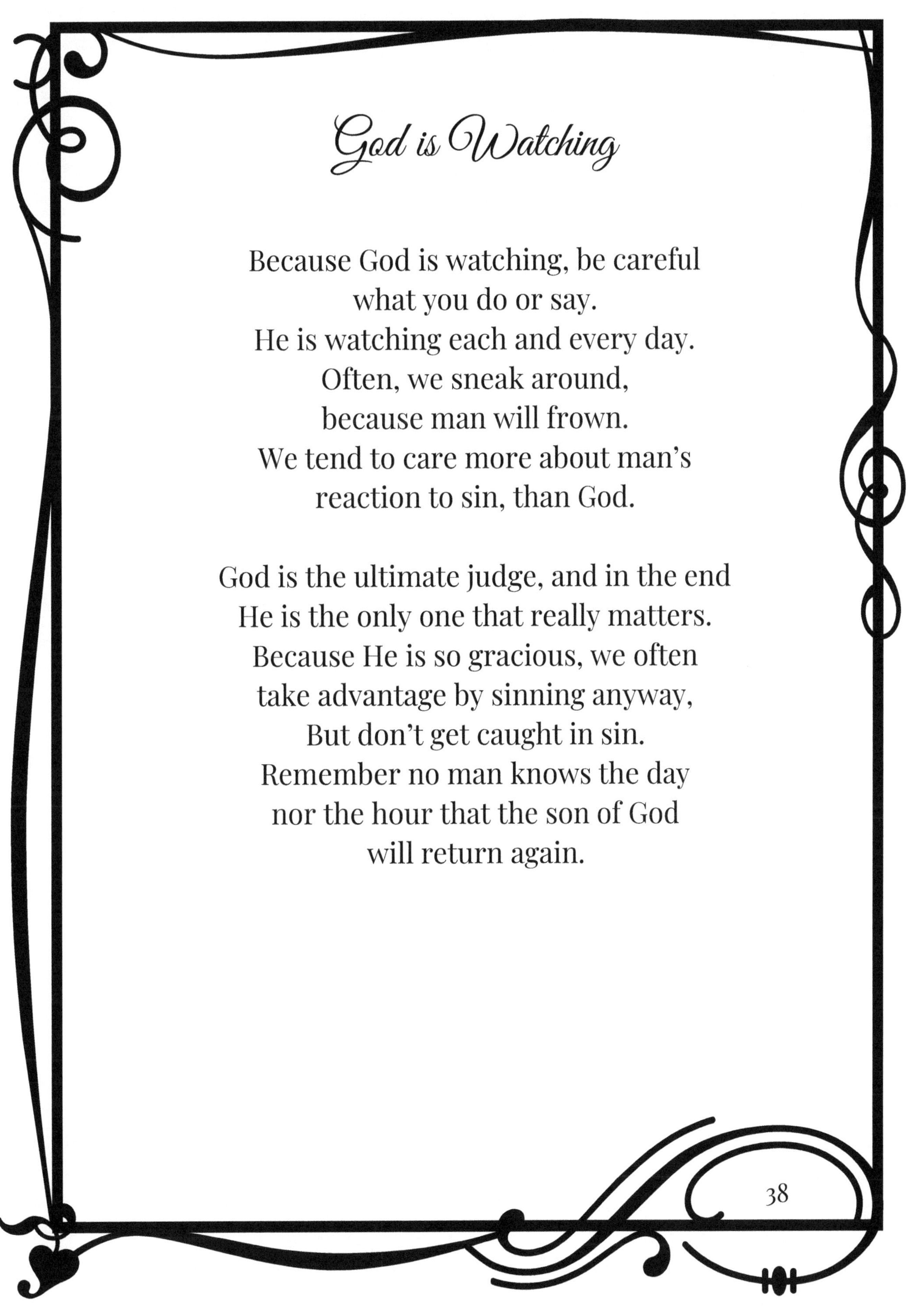

God is Watching

Because God is watching, be careful
what you do or say.
He is watching each and every day.
Often, we sneak around,
because man will frown.
We tend to care more about man's
reaction to sin, than God.

God is the ultimate judge, and in the end
He is the only one that really matters.
Because He is so gracious, we often
take advantage by sinning anyway,
But don't get caught in sin.
Remember no man knows the day
nor the hour that the son of God
will return again.

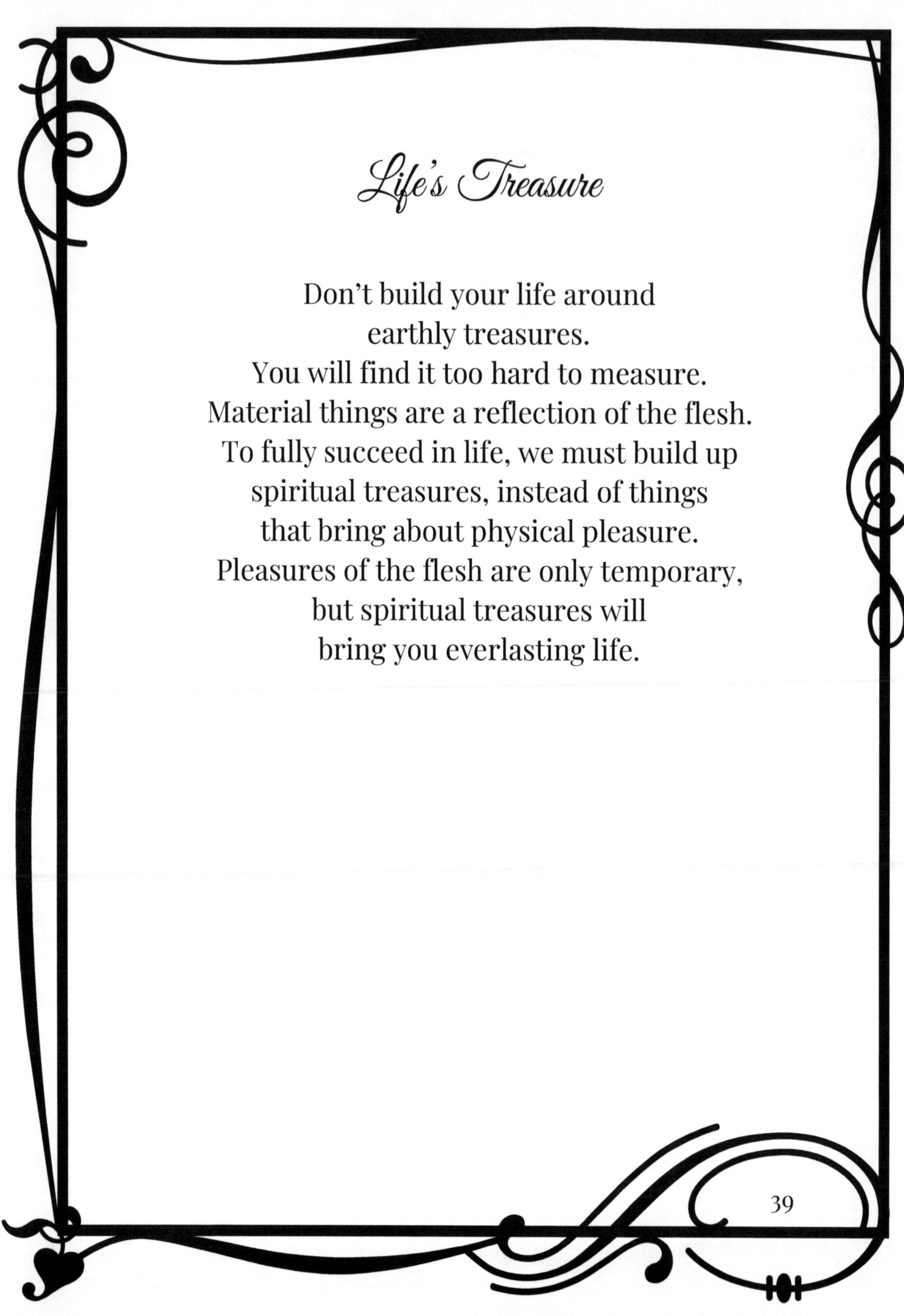

Life's Treasure

Don't build your life around
earthly treasures.
You will find it too hard to measure.
Material things are a reflection of the flesh.
To fully succeed in life, we must build up
spiritual treasures, instead of things
that bring about physical pleasure.
Pleasures of the flesh are only temporary,
but spiritual treasures will
bring you everlasting life.

Patience is a virtue, endure it.

Chapter 5

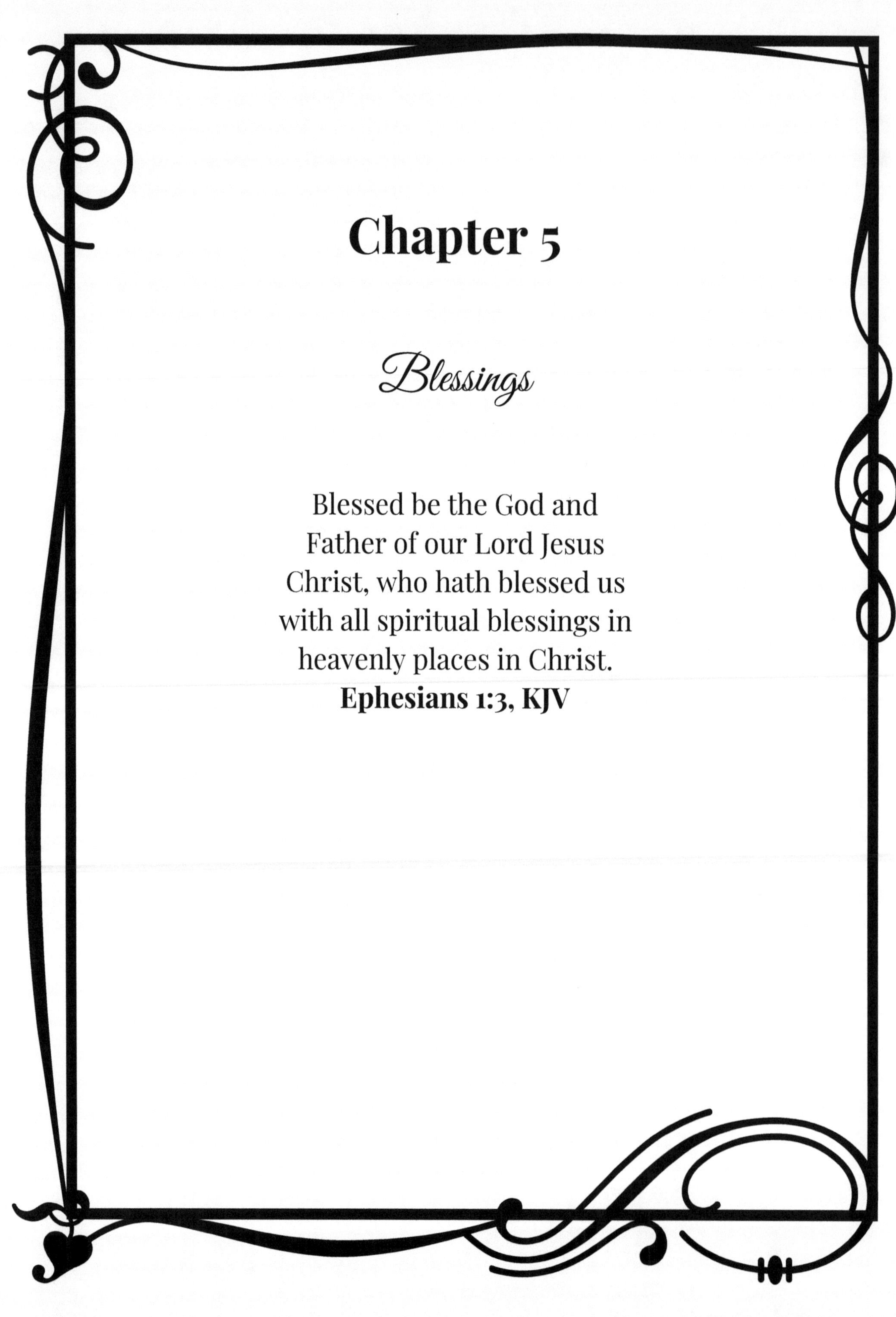

Blessings

Blessed be the God and
Father of our Lord Jesus
Christ, who hath blessed us
with all spiritual blessings in
heavenly places in Christ.
Ephesians 1:3, KJV

Let it Rain

Clouds in the sky,
I don't have to ask why.
Rain is on the way.
To complain,
would be insane,
because the sight of rain
is a good thing.
This is not a waterfall,
but a shower of blessings,
free for all.
Let it rain,
I'm all for the gain.
Let it rain, let it pour
I welcome all blessings,
expecting more and more.

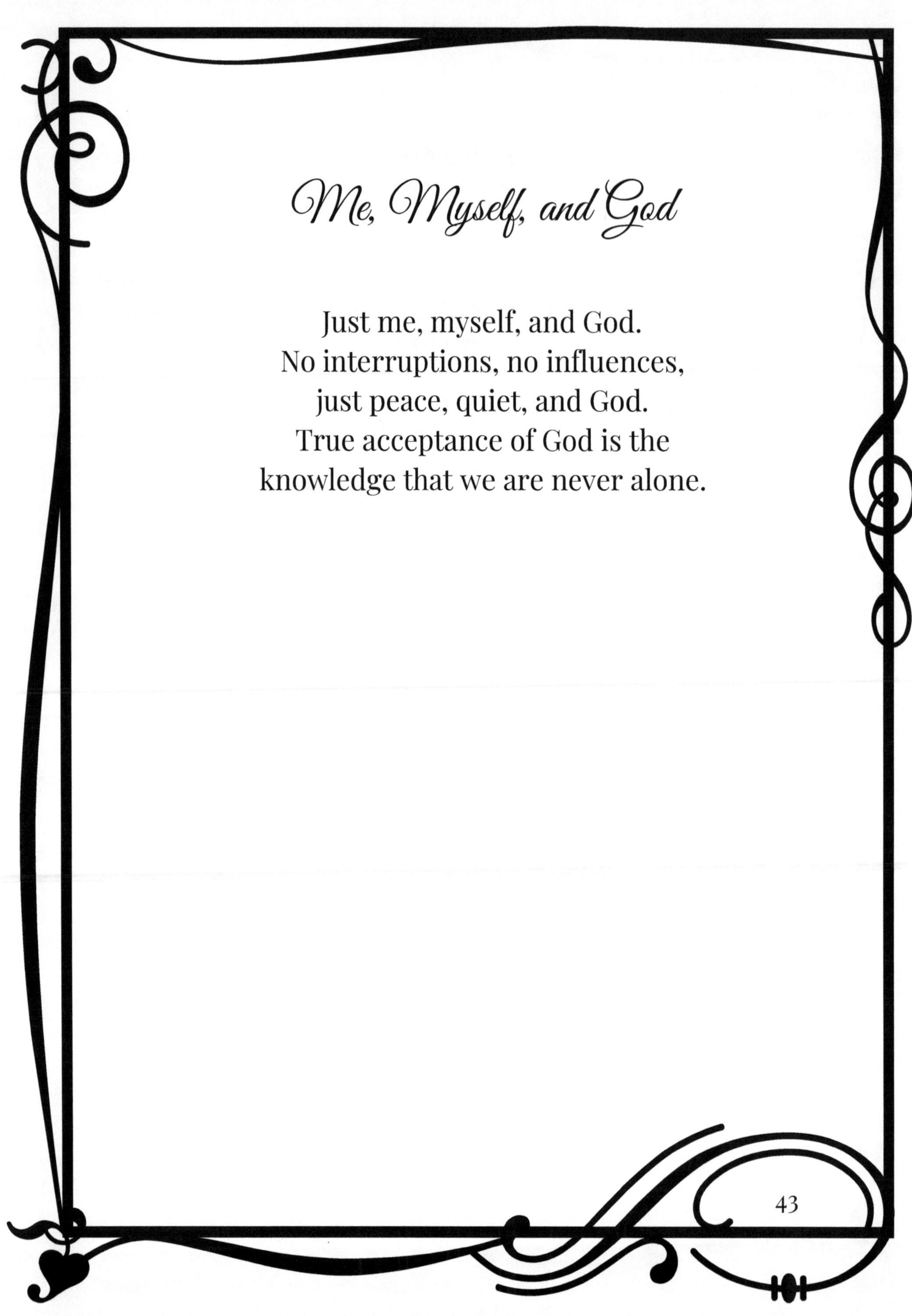

Me, Myself, and God

Just me, myself, and God.
No interruptions, no influences,
just peace, quiet, and God.
True acceptance of God is the
knowledge that we are never alone.

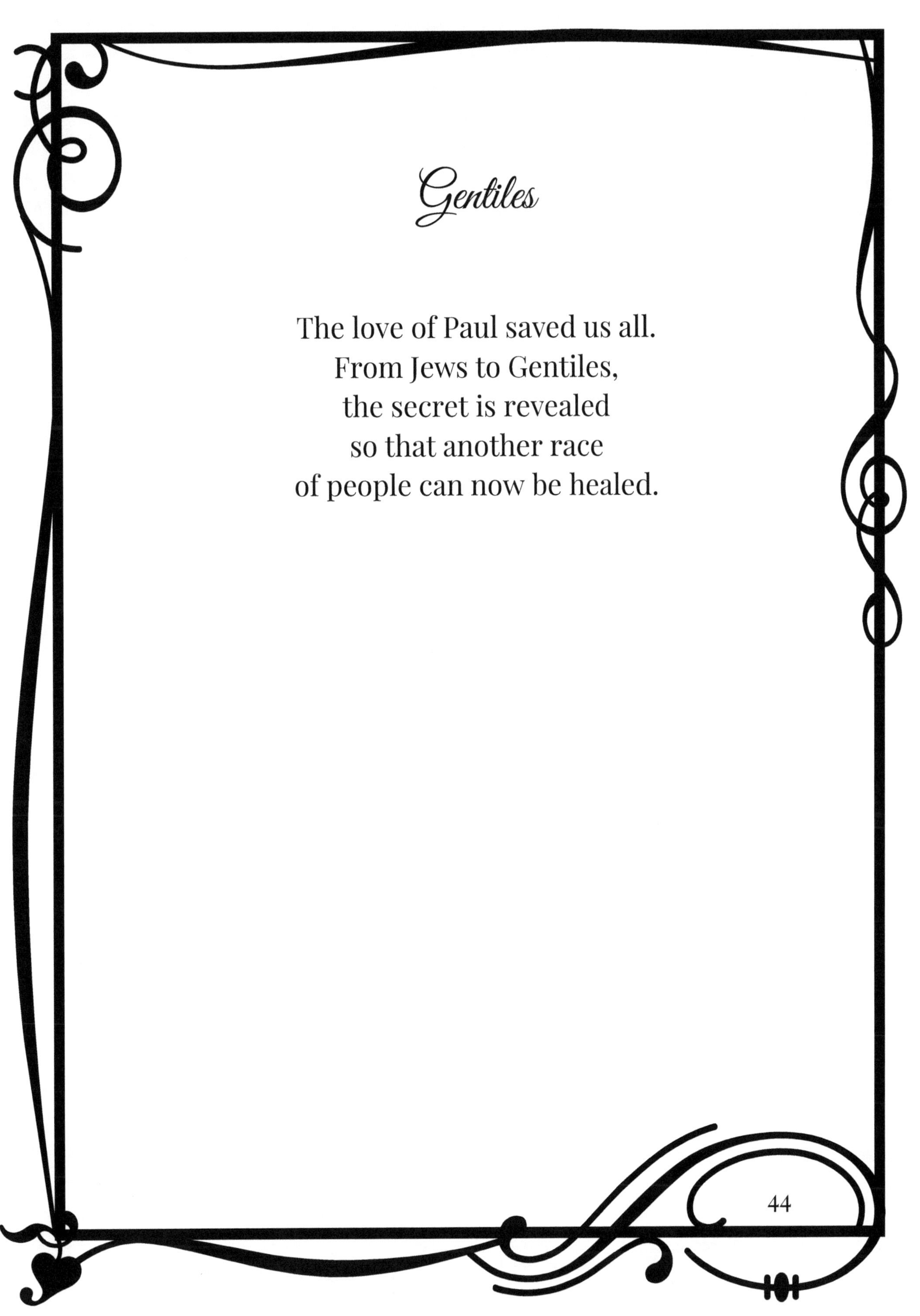

Gentiles

The love of Paul saved us all.
From Jews to Gentiles,
the secret is revealed
so that another race
of people can now be healed.

God made a Way

The only reason that I am here today,
is because God made a way.
He loved me when I couldn't
love myself.
God made sure that I was encouraged,
which could have only been heaven sent.
Because God never gave up on me,
makes it easy for me to say,
I know God will always
make a way.

The Tulip

Tulips are large showy flowers
with bright colors.
They come in a rainbow of colors,
sizes, and flower forms.
The basic meaning of a tulip
is perfect love.
Colors of tulips differ in the
many aspects of love.
Just as we are all of different
colors, sizes, and forms, we are
all covered by God's perfect love.

**Your enemies you must ignore,
be an eagle and continue to soar.**

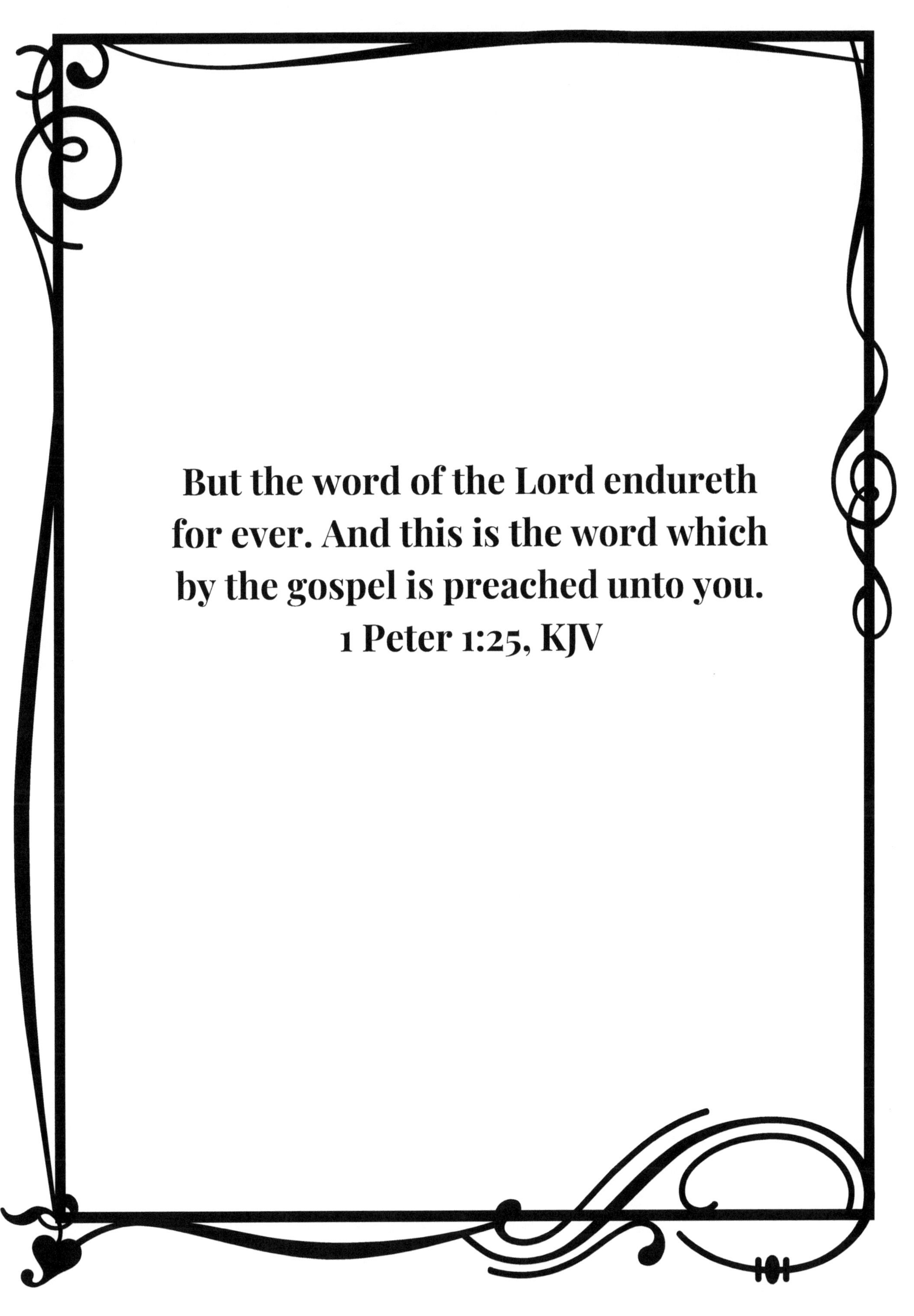

But the word of the Lord endureth
for ever. And this is the word which
by the gospel is preached unto you.
1 Peter 1:25, KJV